Break Ungodly Soul Ties

Who or what is tied to your Soul?

Study Guide By: Mary Favors

Break Ungodly Soul Ties   ISBN- **978-1-4507-6361-5**
www.divinefavorsbooks.com **or**   Email: divinefavorsbks@aol.com
Divine Favors Publication
P.O. Box 44722
Atlanta, GA 30336

It's Your Time, Published your book(s) with DFCP

References: Hebrew, Greek Septuagint. Laint Vulgate, Wycliffe Version, King James, Version, American Standard Version, World English Version, Wikipedia Encyclopedia, Amplified Version, Matthew Henry's Concise Commentary on the Bible, Art Scroll is an imprint of translations, books and commentaries from an Orthodox Jewish perspective published by Mesorah Publications, Ltd., a publishing company based in Brooklyn, New York. Its general editors are Rabbis Nosson Scherman and Meir Zlotowitz, Merriam- Webster dictionary definition, Holman Bible Dictionary, Webster Dictionary, New International Version, Amplified, New American Standard The Prophet's Dictionary, Wikipedia Encyclopedia

Printed in the United States of America

Preface

God Loves You!

The Bible says, "God so loved the world that He gave His one and only Son, that whoever believes in Him shall not perish, but have eternal life"

The problem is that . . .

All of us have done, said or thought things that are wrong. This is called sin, and our sins have separated us from God.

The Bible says "All have sinned and fall short of the glory of God." God is perfect and holy, and our sins separate us from God forever. The Bible says "The wages of sin is death."

The good news is that, about 2,000 years ago,

God sent His only Son Jesus Christ to die for our sins.

Jesus is the Son of God. He lived a sinless life and then died on the cross to pay the penalty for our sins. "God demonstrates His own love for us in that while we were yet sinners Christ died for us."

Jesus rose from the dead and now He lives in heaven with God His Father. He offers us the gift of eternal life -- of living forever with Him in heaven if we accept Him as our Lord and Savior. Jesus said "I am the way, the truth, and the life. No one comes to the Father except by Me."

God reaches out in love to you and wants you to be His child. "As many as received Him, to them He gave the right to become children of God, even to those who believe on His name." You can choose to ask Jesus Christ to forgive your sins and come in to your life as your Lord and Savior.

Are you a Christian? Yes or No
If you answer no or if you are not sure;
I ask you to become part of the family of Christ.

Receive Jesus as Savior and Lord
Prayer of Salvation

"Father God I come to you in the name of Your son Jesus Christ. It is written in Your Word, that if I confess with my mouth Jesus as Lord and believe in my heart that You have raised Him from the dead, I shall be saved. Therefore, Father, I confess that Jesus is my Lord. I make Him Lord of my life right now. I believe in my heart that You raised Jesus from the dead, I renounce my past life with Satan.

"I ask You and thank You for forgiving me of all my sin. Jesus is my Lord, and I am a new creation. Old things have passed away. Now all things become new in Jesus' name. Amend."

Read and Write Scripture Reference

John 3:16
John 6:37
John 10:10b
Romans 3:23
II Corinthians 5:19
John 16:8, 9
Romans 5:8

John 14:6
Romans 10:9-10
Romans10:13
Ephesians 2:1-10
II Corinthians 5:17
John 1:12
II Corinthians 5:21

John 3:16

_____
_____
_____
_____
_____
_____

John 14:6

_____
_____
_____
_____
_____
_____
_____
_____

John 6:37

_____
_____
_____
_____

Romans 10:9-10

_____
_____
_____
_____
_____
_____
_____

John 10:10b

_____
_____
_____

Romans10:13

_____
_____
_____
_____
_____

Romans 3:23

_____

_____

_____

_____

Ephesians 2:1-10

_____

_____

_____

_____

_____

_____

_____

_____

_____

_____

_____

_____

_____

_____

_____

_____

_____

_____

_____

_____

_____

_____

_____

_____

II Corinthians 5:19

_____

_____

_____

_____

_____

II Corinthians 5:17

_____

_____

_____

_____

_____

John 16:8, 9

_____

_____

_____

_____

_____

_____

_____

_____

_____

_____

_____

_____

_____

John 1:12

_____
_____
_____
_____
_____
_____
_____

Romans 5:8

_____
_____
_____
_____
_____
_____

II Corinthians 5:21

_____
_____
_____
_____
_____
_____
_____
_____

Prayer for Spiritual Wisdom and Revelation of God's Word

I Pray that God of our Lord Jesus Christ, the Father of glory, may give me the spirit of wisdom and revelation in the knowledge of Him, and the eyes of my understanding being enlightened; that I may know what is the hope of His calling, what are the riches of the glory of His inheritance in the saints, and what *is* the exceeding greatness of His power toward us who believe, according to the working of His mighty power which He worked in Christ when He raised Him from the dead and seated *Him* at His right hand in the heavenly *places,* far above all principality and power and might and dominion, and every name that is named, not only in this age but also in that which is to come. And He put all *things* under His feet, and gave Him *to be* head over all *things* to the church, which is His body, the fullness of Him who fills all in all.

Thank You Father God; for spiritual wisdom and revelation of Your Word in Jesus' name. Amen

Prayer to receive the Infilling of the Holy Spirit

"Heavenly Father, I come to you in the name of Jesus Christ. I believe in my heart that Jesus has been raised from the dead and I have confessed Him as my Lord.

Jesus said, "How much more shall your heavenly Father give the Holy Spirit to those that ask Him. I ask You now in the name of Jesus to fill me with the Holy Spirit. I step into the fullness and power that I desire in the name of Jesus. I confess that I am a Spirit-filled Christian. As I yield my vocal organs, I expect to speak in tongues for the Spirit gives me utterance in the name of Jesus. "Praise the Lord!"

Scripture Reference Read and Write them.

John 14:16, 17	Acts 10: 44-46
Luke 11:13	Acts 19:2, 5, 6,
Acts 1:8a	I Corinthians 14:2-15
Acts 2:4	I Corinthians 14:18, 27
Acts 2:32, 33, 39	Ephesians 6:18
Acts 8: 12-17	Jude 1:20

Scripture Reference: Read and Write

John 14:16, 17

_____
_____
_____
_____
_____
_____

Luke 11:13

_____
_____
_____

Acts 1:8a

_____
_____
_____

Acts 2:4

_____
_____
_____
_____
_____
_____

Scripture Reference: Read and Write

Acts 2:32, 33, 39

_____

_____

_____

_____

_____

_____

_____

_____

Acts 8: 12-17

_____

_____

_____

_____

_____

_____

_____

_____

_____

_____

_____

_____

_____

_____

_____

Scripture Reference: Read and Write

Acts 10: 44-46

_____

_____

_____

_____

_____

_____

_____

_____

_____

_____

_____

Acts 19:2, 5, 6

_____

_____

_____

_____

_____

_____

_____

_____

_____

Scripture Reference: Read and Write

I Corinthians 14:2-15

_____

_____

_____

_____

_____

_____

_____

_____

_____

_____

_____

_____

_____

_____

_____

_____

_____

_____

_____

_____

_____

_____

_____

_____

_____

_____

_____

_____

Scripture Reference: Read and Write

Ephesians 6:18

_____

_____

_____

_____

_____

_____

_____

_____

Jude 1:20

_____

_____

_____

_____

_____

_____

_____

_____

_____

John 10:10
The thief cometh not, but for to steal, and to kill, and to destroy: I am come that they might have **life**, and that they might have it **more abundantly**.

Jesus came that you may have an abundantly life.

This day will you choose life? You cannot move forward with God if you cannot resolve the things of the past. Whatever you are lost in thought with in your mind, and meditate on those things all the time, and cannot hear the voice of the Holy Spirit, your soul is probably tied to something or someone.

The Lord had you to read this book for a reason. He loves you so much He always wants the best for you.

Your Own Thoughts and Reflection

Chapter 1

What Is Soul Ties?

WHAT IS "SOUL TIE"?

The King James version uses three words (knit, cleave, and bound up) that all have the same meaning according to Strong's Exhaustive Concordance of being "cling or adhere", "abide fast, fast together, follow close, be joined, keep, stick." The Lord uses good or godly soul ties to strengthen relationships, to hold us together, if you will. Let's take a look at the Bible.

A soul tie is the joining or knitting together of the bonds of a relationship. Godly soul ties occur when like-minded believers are together in the Lord: friends, marriage partners, believers to pastors, etc.

Relationships that lack 'God-centeredness' can result in ungodly soul ties between friends, parents and children, siblings, marriage partners, former romantic or sexual partners, domineering authorities, etc.

An unhealthy attachment with another can bring about a psychic control that can adversely affect the life, e.g. a mother who refuses to relinquish her hold on her children (tied to her apron strings), a person who refuses to release to the Lord the memory of an old romantic flame (withdrawing into nostalgia in times of loneliness), a person who holds a grudge or a judgment against another, someone who uses spiritual forces to control others (witchcraft), etc."
For two people to bond to the point of a soul tie often takes time, particularly in the area of friendships.

Man's soul consists of his mind, emotions, and will. A soul tie involves the joining of minds, ideas and views, as well as emotional unions in the feeling realm. Soul ties can range from being laid back and fairly loose to quite intense and overpowering. For example, think of a piece of thread, a string, a rope, and finally, a length of cable. Each tie is progressively stronger than the one before. A 'thread' relationship would simply be an acquaintance, someone you greet at your job every day. You know their name and where they work, but that's about it. A 'string' relationship would perhaps be an associate who you're more intellectually tied to, someone with whom you have certain things in common.

A **rope relationship** would be a good friend, a companion and confidant, one in whom you would be free to 'be yourself' and share things about your life that are somewhat vulnerable.

Finally, a **cable relationship** would be someone to whom you're related: your wife, your kids, and your immediate family.

Now, breaking a piece of thread is not difficult. In the same way, losing a casual acquaintance is not a big deal emotionally. Breaking a string may take some effort, and so the loss of an associate would affect you to some degree, depending on the depth and length of the relationship. A rope or a cable, however, would require tremendous exertion to break, particularly if there was tension in the line. So it is that the loss of an intimate friend or family member can affect your soul tremendously. Healthy soul ties stabilize the soul. The more you open up to the intimacies involved in relationships, the more you experience the freedom to be yourself. Let's consider healthy and godly type soul ties described in the Bible:

Your Own Thoughts and Reflection

What is the difference between the soul and the spirit?

We are a spirit being, we live in a body and we possess a soul. The real person inside of us is our spirit. Our soul consists of our mind, will and emotions. Our bodies are the temple in which we live.

When we are born again, we are linked to Christ through the spirit.

1 Cor. 6:17 *"But he that is joined unto the Lord is one spirit."* You receive the mind of Christ by having your mind renewed by the Spirit of God and coming to the place of having ears to hear what the spirit speaks to you.

In the garden, Adam was not controlled by his soul and did not live in the soulish realm. Because His spirit was united with the Lord, He truly walked in the spirit and ruled from His spirit, and was not controlled by the will or dictates of His soul.

After the fall, man's spirit died, it lost its unity of being joined to the Lord and was now joined to the devil. Everything your flesh loves, Satan loves. Everything your flesh hates, Satan hates. Man's fallen nature is married to the things of the god of this world. You don't have to teach a child to be selfish, to steal or anything that is wrong. You have to train them not to do evil. Much of what you are doing with a child is soul training because until we come to the place of being born again of the spirit of God, we are controlled and live by our flesh and its dictates.

The only reason that some don't do the evil things many others do is because they have accepted that soul training and accepted the laws and rules of society. One of the problems today is many children are not receiving that soul training they need to be responsible adults. We are not morally good because we are born good. We are all born with a fallen sinful nature. When we are born again, the battle between the soul and spirit begins. That's Romans 6-7

So how do demonic spirits vex and possess people? It is through their souls, and their bodies.

An example of a bodily demonic affliction is: *Luke 13:11, "And, behold, there was a woman which had a spirit of infirmity eighteen years, and was bowed together, and could in no wise lift up herself."*

An example of a mental demonic affliction we call being demon possessed: *Matthew 17:15,18, "Lord, have mercy on my son: for he is lunatic, and sore vexed: for ofttimes he falleth into the fire, and oft into the water... And Jesus rebuked the devil; and he departed out of him: and the child was cured from that very hour."*

Our souls were not born again!

The Bible is clear that even though our spirits are born again, our mind, will and emotions still need to be cleansed. Being born of the spirit and the saving of the soul are two different things.

1 Peter 1:22-23 "Seeing ye have purified your souls in obeying the truth through the Spirit ... Being born again, not of corruptible seed, but of incorruptible, by the word of God, which liveth and abideth forever."

Our spirit is instantly reborn the moment we accept Christ as our Lord and savior, but our souls have to be transformed by the renewing of our minds to the Word of God, according to *Romans 12:2.*

Our souls can carry over much spiritual defilement from our past lifestyles. Because their soul still contains defilements that need to be washed clean, many believers can continue to struggle with sin even after accepting Christ.

Your Own Thoughts and Reflection

_____

_____

_____

_____

_____

_____

_____

_____

_____

_____

_____

_____

_____

_____

_____

_____

_____

The Soul in opposition to The Spirit:

We must not let our soul rule us. The soul will always try to be in control and that is why it is of the utmost importance to feed our spirit with the Word of God, worship and prayer.

A spiritual principle is this, "What you feed grows, what you starve dies. You don't satisfy anything by feeding it; you only increase its capacity to grow." So, what are you feeding the most, your spiritual man or your flesh by worldly things and entertainment?

Gal.5:16 *"This I say then, Walk in the Spirit, and ye shall not fulfill the lust of the flesh."* God wants us to be free from any and all types of bondages of the enemy. Ungodly soul ties have kept many from the destinies that God has ordained for them. The ungodly ties have suppressed the eternal purposes of God, and frustrated plans for many believers who want to serve God. Many are hiding behind a mask, but behind the mask are hurt, discouragement and broken hearts. The pain is hidden on the outside, but it is very real on the inside. It is time to take off the mask, be honest and get free.

An ungodly soul tie is when the mind, will and emotions of a person becomes entangled to the point where their thoughts are not always their own, when a person is unnaturally affected by the will, the emotions and desires of someone or something else. You can also be soul-tied to things. When things in your life are keeping you from doing what God has called you to do, it is an ungodly tie. He wants you to have good things but He does not want things to have your heart.

SPIRIT, SOUL AND BODY - The human being is composed of eternal spirit, intellectual soul and fleshly body. God imparted the spirit into the womb at the moment of conception. The soul is normally thought of as mind, will and emotions. The soul and body are grown as we develop as humans. When we die, God will take our spirit and soul into the spiritual world leaving our fleshly body behind. We will recognize each other when we get to Heaven because we will have our souls, which contain our memory.

An animal is composed of soul and body but no spirit. When the animal dies, there is no indication in the Bible that God preserves any part of the animal or that any earthly animals will be found in heaven. There are heavenly animals that are there now, such as horses, and will probably be there when we arrive.

Demons have a spirit and soul but do not have a body.

When we unite with another, we unite in the soul. A demonic tie is formed between men and women depending on what the union is all about. A soul tie or some form of demonic tie may be formed with beasts, demons and objects.

Note:

When you see what does the Bible say about_____?

Get your Bible and look up scriptures and write the scriptures down.

SOUL TIES - Soul ties are simply becoming one flesh according to the Bible; the souls are united. Soul ties are invisible ties between live humans, live humans and animals, live humans and dead humans. Soul ties between live humans would include husband and wife, man and whore, woman and gigolo, man and man, and woman and woman. Soul ties between humans and animals would include sex with animals by men or women. Soul ties between live humans and dead humans would include any inability to give up the dead or influence of the dead on the living.

Have you been married before and divorced or separated? Is your former mate dead? If so, you have a soul tie with that person that needs to be broken unless you plan to reunite with that person after temporary separation.

What does the Bible say about soul ties?

_____

_____

_____

_____

_____

_____

_____

_____

_____

_____

_____

GODLY SOUL TIES - There is a good soul tie between godly married mates. God established this as one of His Laws. My wife and I have a godly soul tie. This is our only marriage and we do not have any other former mates. We are one flesh. We became one flesh when we united in sex. Marriage in the Bible was consummated when the couple came together sexually. They simply went into the tent, had sex and they were married in the sight of God. There is no need for paperwork or formalities in the sight of God; these are needed for man's world.

What does the Bible say about godly soul ties?

_____

_____

_____

_____

_____

_____

_____

_____

_____

_____

_____

_____

_____

_____

FORNICATION AND ADULTERY - Fornication is all sexual acts outside of godly marriage union. Fornication would include sex between men and women before marriage even if the consenting adults got married after sex. Most people think that if they get married after a child is conceived, it is not illegitimate. In the sight of God, the child is a bastard.

A soul tie is formed immediately upon the sexual act. God made the woman to have a strong attraction to the first man that she had sex with. It is going to be very difficult for the woman to forget her first sexual partner even when she gets married to another man. She may want to go back to her first partner as she goes through life.

Adultery is ungodly sexual acts in marriage with another person. Adultery is also defined as fornication. If a man or woman has sex outside of marriage with another, then a soul tie is formed with that person. When the married person goes to bed with their godly mate, it is as if they were bringing the other people to bed with them. This explains why people have some problems with their sex lives. They think about others during this time.

Sex with the harlot, whore, and prostitute gigolo (either male or female) causes a soul tie to be formed just the same as if the marriage was legitimate before God. Any soul tie outside of marriage is ungodly.

The world gets caught in the age-old trap of thinking that sex is love. Sex is not love; sex is sex. Sex in marriage should be sex with love but may only be sex without love. This may be brought about by the wife bargaining for sex with the husband to get something she wants or for some other reason.

What does the Bible say about FORNICATION AND ADULTERY?

_____

_____

_____

_____

_____

_____

_____

_____

_____

_____

_____

_____

_____

_____

_____

_____

_____

_____

_____

_____

HOMOSEXUALITY - Homosexuality forms soul ties between men and men or women and women. They have united their souls through the sexual act of sodomy. There is now a spiritual tie between them similar to the ties of being married.

What does the Bible say about homosexuality?

_____
_____
_____
_____
_____
_____
_____
_____
_____
_____
_____
_____
_____
_____
_____
_____
_____
_____
_____
_____

BESTIALITY - Bestiality is the sexual union between man or woman and beast. It may be that a soul tie is formed between the person and the beast. Have you noticed that some people treat their animals as if they were their children? Why do people have an ungodly attraction for animals? It is probably not all for bestiality but it illustrates how a person can be attracted to animals as if they were humans.

What does the Bible say about bestiality?

_____

_____

_____

_____

_____

_____

_____

_____

_____

_____

_____

_____

_____

_____

_____

_____

_____

_____

CURSES - Curses are a type of demonic tie between the living, and between the living and the dead. Curses speak of oaths, binding and lying upon. God can curse us for not following His Laws. We can curse ourselves and bind ourselves under a curse. We can curse others and bind them under a curse if we have the authority to do so (such as our children).

When the curse is broken, there is a release as if a tie had been severed. I have always wanted to see the connection in the spiritual world of the curse emanating from someone and landing on someone else. We can curse ourselves or others can curse us. How does the release occur? Is the tie suddenly severed or does the demon suddenly leave or what really happens? I wish God would open my eyes so that I could see into the spiritual world and see what happens there. I would like to see what happens as we pray war in the spirit world, etc. Practicing deliverance is the best education that I know of to help you see into the spiritual world and understand what happens.

What does the Bible say about curse?

_____

_____

_____

_____

_____

_____

_____

_____

_____

_____

_____

_____

_____

_____

_____

_____

_____

_____

_____

_____

_____

_____

_____

_____

_____

_____

_____

_____

WITCHCRAFT - Witchcraft is the attempt to exercise control over others for personal gain. It can be practiced by white witchcraft (so called good witchcraft), black witchcraft (evil witchcraft), or someone who doesn't even think that they are a witch. Someone would practice deliberate witchcraft in the occult or Satan worship. You don't have to be a witch or warlock to practice witchcraft.

When we go to a witch to gain hidden knowledge or something for ourselves, we are seeking to them as we would seek to God. We are submitting ourselves to them, become obligated to them and they begin to exercise control over us.

Someone trying to control others for their benefit or even for good intentions would practice witchcraft unknowingly. Parents have a right and responsibility to control children that are underage and are supported by them. Parents do not have the right or responsibility to control children that are of age and are not supported by them especially when they are married.

Laymen and leaders commonly practice witchcraft unknowingly in the Christian world. This is called charismatic witchcraft. A pastor or leader who tries to control his flock or group is practicing witchcraft. He or she may feel that they know what is best for their people and they try to force it to happen. They may or may not know what is best for others but they have no right to force their will on others. The best example is God will not force His Will on us.

We have worked with people who have been controlled by a dictatorial pastor. The pastor has formed soul ties with those who have yielded to his control rather than the direction of God in their lives. It is necessary to forgive the pastor, break soul ties and cast out demons.

If you have left a church that truly does not follow Jesus Christ, then you need to renounce that church or organization, forgive them, break soul ties, and cast out demons. The Catholic Church is a good example of an organization that tries to control their people completely. Many charismatic leaders fall into this trap of trying to control people and their money in order to build their kingdoms whether small or large.

We went to a church where the pastor seemed to let the Holy Spirit have His way in the services. There was a tremendous freedom there and you could hardly wait to get to church to see what God was going to do. Then the pastor decided that it was his church and would be run the way he wanted it to be run for his selfish reasons. After that, the freedom left and it was like any other charismatic church.

If you went to a fortune teller to get your fortune told, then you formed a soul tie with that person. There will be an attempt to control your life by that person from then on. Attempted control forms a soul tie. Demons will be sent out to help you and to draw you back to the fortune teller. God will cut us off. He may kill us as He did Saul for seeking the medium. He may cut us off from His Blessings on us mentally, physically, spiritually or materially. God places you in bondage. You may lose your mind, health, wealth or relationship with God. You are cursed and God may put ties on you to prevent you from prospering.

Witchcraft causes demons to be sent to another person to affect their life. The demons may stay on the outside of the person and just talk to the person or may affect their material surroundings. The demons may converse with the demons within the person and get their co-operation for your destruction.

What does the Bible say about witchcraft?

_____

_____

_____

_____

_____

_____

_____

_____

_____

_____

_____

_____

_____

_____

_____

_____

BANDS - There are bands that bind us. These demonic ties are bands, bonds, fetters, cords, ropes, covenants, brotherhoods, etc. that have strength, might and force over our lives.

We have worked with people in deliverance who acted like they had bands around their heads or bonds around their bodies. There would be pressure on their heads as if something was tightened around their skull or brain. Similarly, there might be a feeling of pressure around the body or organ.

What does the Bible say about bands?

_____

_____

_____

_____

_____

_____

_____

_____

_____

_____

_____

_____

_____

_____

_____

COVENANTS - We have cut a covenant with Jesus Christ. He has given us all of His Benefits and we have given Him all of our life. This is a blood covenant founded on the Blood of Jesus Christ. This is a very serious agreement and should not be taken lightly.

Beauty is symbolic name given to one of the two staves, which symbolized the Lords' covenant with the seed of Jacob, and the brotherhood of Israel and Judah. I would say that this word symbolizes the good things that God will do for us.

Bands are a symbolic name given to the other of the two staves mentioned above. Strong's lists the following for bands: twisted rope, measuring line, inheritance, noose, cord, tied together, ruin, destruction, pain, pang, snare, sorrow. I would say that this word symbolizes the bad things that God will do to us. It could also mean that God sets a measuring line for us not to go past and that is our inheritance in Him. If we exceed His limits, then we face ruin, destruction, pain, pang, snare and sorrow. We could be twisted like a rope, have a noose around our neck and tied together with a cord.

David agreed with Jonathan to be his brother. They treated each other as if they were blood brothers. This agreement lasted after the dead of Jonathan. David was obligated to care for the descendents of Saul and Jonathan. David lived up to his agreement. Are you living up to your agreement with God?

What does the Bible say about covenants?

_____

_____

_____

_____

_____

_____

_____

_____

_____

_____

_____

_____

_____

_____

_____

_____

_____

_____

_____

_____

_____

_____

_____

_____

_____

_____

_____

BROTHERHOODS - Have you joined a brotherhood outside of Christianity? Have you agreed to or signed a document that causes you to treat those in that organization as if they were your blood brothers or sisters? An example would be the Masons. Have you ever cut your wrist, mingled your blood with another, drunk mingled blood and wine out of a chalice such as an Indian rite?

As Christians, we are brothers and sisters in Christ by His Blood. We are a family and may form some strong ties which may seem even stronger than those with our blood brothers and sisters who turn against us as we follow the Lord. This needs to be a natural love and not a contrived false love. Calling someone brother or sister does not indicate that you really mean it but may just be putting on a show.

What does the Bible say about brotherhood out side of Christianity?

_____
_____
_____
_____
_____
_____
_____
_____
_____

YOKE OF BONDAGE - Have you ever felt that you have a yoke of iron upon your neck or that you were carrying a heavy load on your back or that you felt a heaviness on you? This feeling could be analogous to having bands around you. It can come about because you did not serve THE LORD YOUR GOD with joyfulness and gladness of heart.

What does the Bible say about yoke?

_____
_____
_____
_____
_____
_____
_____
_____
_____
_____
_____
_____
_____
_____
_____
_____
_____
_____
_____

SPIRITUAL STRENGTH, MIGHT AND FORCE

Many Christians act as if there was no force in the spiritual world either good or evil. They may act as if God had no power or would not exercise that power in the lives of men. They may act as if Satan had no power or could not exercise that power over them.

God is all powerful, all knowing and all present - omnipotent, omniscient, omnipresent. God exercises those qualities in our lives whether we realize it or not.

Satan is the second most powerful being in the universe, only second to God - Father, Son and Holy Spirit. He and his forces can do demonic miracles to fool men. Except for Jesus Christ on our side, we are powerless before him. With Jesus Christ on our side, we have all power over the enemy.

You may act as if Satan was a buffoon or wore a red suit with a tail and carried a pitchfork. You need to know your enemy. It is Satan and his forces, not man that is causing you problems. Satan has one-third of the angels, billions of demons and about 98% of the human race in his army. We don't need to fear this mighty enemy but we need to respect his power and learn how to overcome the enemy's army.

What does the Bible say about a Christian SPIRITUAL STRENGTH, MIGHT in JESUS?

_____

_____

_____

_____

_____

_____

_____

_____

_____

_____

_____

_____

_____

_____

_____

_____

_____

_____

_____

_____

_____

_____

_____

TYPES OF CATEGORIES

This list would include any demons that would cause demonic ties of any type. They include general categories of sexual unions, people who would control your freewill, you practicing witchcraft on others, and demonic ties to objects, animals and demons. Demonic ties could be thought of as holds over your life or being tied to something that you can not let go of. You are tied to anything that has a hold over some aspect of your life. What do you worship and what is important in your life; this is a key to your ties.

Demonic ties can be caused by parents abusing their children causing them to try to please them and gain their acceptance for the rest of their adult lives. They can be caused by weak effeminate men and strong domineering women improperly raising their children. Ties can be caused by false religions or religious leaders. Addictions are a type of tie to drugs, alcohol, food, etc. Children can have demonic ties with their parents as well as godly ties. You can be tied to your enemies because of your hatred and inability to release them from their sins against you. You can be tied to worldly systems of religion, family, occupation, education, recreation, etc. You can be tied to races, cultures and creeds. You can be tied to doctors and hospitals for treatment of body and mind. You can be tied to yourself through selfishness and only thinking about your needs. You can be tied to traditions of your elders or churches.

You can be tied to medium spirits, which guide your life, or to your own demons that you submit to. Familiar spirits following the descendents after the ancestor's sins could be a type of tie. You can even be tied to someone that has died. You can be tied to the Devil through occult, witchcraft and Satan worship. You can be tied to demons that you have sex with.

What does the Bible say about occult and witchcraft?

_____

_____

_____

_____

_____

_____

_____

_____

_____

_____

_____

_____

_____

_____

_____

_____

_____

MARRIAGE SOUL TIES

The first mention of a "soul tie" in the Word is found early in Genesis

Read and Write Genesis 2:21-24

_____

_____

_____

_____

_____

_____

_____

_____

_____

_____

_____

_____

This is the famous "leave and cleave" passage concerning marriage. From the very beginning God's intention has been that the man and woman's soul ties with their parents should be broken prior to marriage. Why is that? Because few things are as destructive to a marriage as when one partner or another is still emotionally tied, and often as a result, manipulated and controlled, by a meddlesome parent. So, interestingly enough, we see that the first Bible reference to a soul tie is an admonition to break a soul tie.

FRIENDSHIP SOUL TIES

Another example is found in the book of Ruth. In fact, this verse is often found in the liturgy of weddings.
Naomi had two sons and two daughter-in-laws. After her sons died, she told her daughter-in-laws they were free to return to their people. One of them, Orpah, did just that. But the other, Ruth, refused to leave. "...Then Orpah kissed her mother-in-law good-by, but Ruth clung to her. "Look," said Naomi, "your
sister-in-law is going back to her people and her gods. Go back with her." But Ruth replied, "Don't urge me to leave you or to turn back from you. Where you go I will go, and where you stay I will stay. Your people will be my people and your God my God. Where you die I will die, and there I will be buried. May the Lord deal with me, severely if need be, if anything but death separates you and me." (Ruth 1:14-17) Ruth was bonded to Naomi like glue. In fact, the Hebrew word for 'clung' (dabaq) is a word similar to the one used in Israel today for 'glue'. So, we see they were "glued together" in a loving and faithful relationship of mother and daughter-in-law.

Read and Write Ruth 1: 14-17

_____

_____

_____

_____

_____

_____

_____

_____

Ruth1: 14-17

Another example of a friendship-type soul tie: "..when he had made an end of speaking to Saul, the soul of Jonathan was knit with the soul of David, and Jonathan loved him as his own soul." (1 Samuel 18:1) Jonathan, the son of King Saul, had great respect and love for David, the future king. The friendship was so deep that we're told their very souls were 'knit' together. This bonding served them both well in the days to come. Jonathan did his best to protect David from Saul's rage and David, when he became king, went to great lengths to care for Jonathan's only remaining son.

Read and Write
1 Sam 18:1

_____

_____

_____

_____

_____

_____

_____

_____

_____

_____

_____

_____

_____

_____

_____

SOUL TIES WITH OTHER BELIEVERS

In these verses you will read and write, believers are encouraged to knit their lives together like threads in a garment, each thread intricately woven with each other thread. This is a picture of how God wants the body of Christ to be. However, soul ties among believers should really be called spirit ties. Believers are 'spirit tied' before they're 'soul tied'. When you experience spiritual rebirth, you become one in Spirit with every other believer. As a result, bonding in the mind and emotions becomes far easier, because of the spirit union already there. This is the reason believers can meet somebody they've never met before and feel like they've known them for many years. Believers "bear witness in their spirit" when they meet someone who loves Jesus. Satan cannot fake real joy or peace. And he particularly cannot counterfeit the love of God that flows spirit to spirit between true believers.

Read and Write 1 Cor. 1:10

_____

_____

_____

_____

_____

_____

_____

_____

_____

Read and Write Col. 2:1-2

_____

_____

_____

_____

_____

_____

_____

_____

_____

_____

It's clear to see the godliness of this act of being "knit together"-having good or godly soul ties. Paul even encourages us in Colossians 2:2 to form godly soul ties with other Christians.

In contrast with this, let's take a look at how the devil has counterfeited this godly bond and perverted it.

*Notes:*_____

_____

_____

_____

_____

_____

_____

_____

_____

_____

SOUL TIES WITH PASTORS OR SPIRITUAL LEADERS

Read and Write 2 Sam. 20:2

_____

_____

_____

_____

_____

_____

_____

_____

_____

Here we see the men of Judah bonding with their leader David. This depicts the soul tie that's needed between believers and their spiritual authorities. Again, the Hebrew word here is 'dabaq' for 'glue'. The men were _glued_ to their authority. We see a similar tie of devotion between Elijah and Elisha, Moses and Joshua and Jesus and His disciples. Such a bond is essential for a pastor or spiritual leader to pass on anointed ministry to those submitted to him in the Lord. There has to be a soul trust - a soul tie that's rooted in a shared passion and sense of vision. As a pastor, I've found this to be true time and again over the years. When such a trust bond was lacking the results were invariably disappointing. But, when I've been privileged to 'have someone's heart', then that person was able to 'catch the vision' and run with it in a way that those without that 'soul trust' could not.

SOUL TIES BETWEEN PARENTS AND CHILDREN

Read and Write Gen. 44:30-31

_____

_____

_____

_____

_____

_____

_____

_____

_____

_____

_____

_____

_____

In this verse, we see a picture of a father so tied with his son that, were his son to fail to appear, he would go down to his grave with sorrow. Few ties are as tight as those between parents and their children, particularly between a mother and her child. God ordained such natural bonding knowing that child rearing is difficult. At times, were it not for such soul ties, many parents might be tempted to give up. But with such ties, a parent can sustain a level of unconditional love essential for the proper development of the child.

PERVERTED FAMILY SOUL TIES

The soul tie between a parent and a child is healthy and beneficial, except when it continues into the adult life of the child. When a son or daughter is ready for marriage, the soul tie with the parents must be terminated in order for a soul tie of marriage to be formed.

When the father gives his daughter in marriage, he severs the soul tie with her in preference to her husband. When the soul tie is not severed between the parent and the child, at the proper time that which was good and beneficial becomes evil through control and possessiveness.

Sexual perverseness within family relations occurs when there is incest between father/daughter, mother/son, brother/sister, father-in-law/daughter-in-law, mother-in-law/son-in-law, or other close family ties.

When the essential bonding between parents and child is missed at birth, the child is left with a sense of incompleteness. This can leave him restless and searching throughout his life. Satan can easily draw such a person into false and perverse soul ties with others.

"When they came to the threshing floor of Arad, which is beyond the Jordan, they lamented there with a very great and sorrowful lamentation; and he observed seven days mourning for his father."
Genesis 50:10

"So the sons of Israel wept for Moses in the plains of Moab thirty days; then the days of weeping and mourning for Moses came to an end.
Deuteronomy 34:8

When a family member or close friend dies, the soul tie formed with that person must be dissolved. The period of sorrow following the death of a loved one is primarily due to the adjustment time during which the soul tie is ended. Prolonged mourning indicates the continuation of the soul tie. This invites spirits of sorrow, grief, loneliness and others to enter.

Your Own Thoughts and Reflection

_____

_____

_____

_____

_____

_____

_____

_____

_____

_____

_____

_____

UNGODLY SOUL TIES

A soul tie is a 'channel'. Think of a soul tie as a soda straw through which flows mental and emotional things. Spiritual things can pass through as well, be they from the human spirit, be they psychically induced, demonically inspired, or genuine and edifying from the Lord. Because demonic spirits can transfer so easily through soul ties, it's essential to identify and destroy those that are ungodly, controlling, or emotionally binding. Let's look at an example of ungodly ties between a father and his sons:

Read and Write 1 Samuel 2:29, 3:13

_____

_____

_____

_____

_____

_____

_____

_____

_____

_____

_____

_____

_____

_____

UNGODLY PATERNAL SOUL TIES

God was rebuking the prophet Eli because of his unwillingness to correct his sons for their sins against the Lord. The sin of Eli was parental permissiveness. As a result, God's judgment came upon his house. In spite of their best efforts, parents can be soul tied to their kids in unhealthy ways. Due to their own insecurities, parents can develop soul ties of indifference, permissiveness, idolatry, compromise and control (and in many other areas). Let's consider some of the symptoms and results of ungodly soul ties between parents and their children.

- ◆ **Symptoms of Unhealthy or Absent Parent / Child Bonding**

- ◆ **Periodically swinging from angry correction to guilt. Manipulative, dishonest in dealings with their child.**

- ◆ **Unreasonably controlling.**

- ◆ **Resistant to counsel concerning their child rearing.**

- ◆ **Defensive for the child when others speak of his / her failings or shortcomings.**

This is always an indicator of a problem: A Sunday School teacher approaches a parent and says, "I'm hesitant to tell you this, but your child has been a real disruption in our class lately." Mom replies, "Not my child! This just can't be true! He's not like that. It must be the effect the other children are having on him." With such words, an unhealthy tie is confirmed.

+ **Unhealthy dependence on the child's part for the parent (often the result of "spoiling").**

One indication of unhealthy dependence is excessive clinginess and crying whenever mom or dad leaves to go somewhere. Often, unhealthy dependence is fostered out of a sense of guilt on the part of the parent. The results can often be as damaging as neglect. God's balance can be seen in nature. As a piece of fruit ripens, so does the tie that connects it to the tree. If you try to remove an apple while it's still green, you'll need to twist and pull to snap it loose. However, when the apple is fully ripe, it will fall off with just the slightest tug. So it should be with children. The dependence that was so essential in the early years needs to gradually give way to a parent-to child respect that will enable them to leave the nest on their own when it's time.

+ **Tendency to yield to the child's manipulation**, thus making consistent discipline difficult.

Allowing the child to dictate and control the parent's activities and relationships. At this point, the soul tie between the parent and child has become quite unhealthy. There's even a passage Isaiah that describes such a state and the curse that goes with it:

Read and Write Isaiah 3:12

Results of Unhealthy or Absent Parent / Child Bonding

Unhealthy (or absent) parent-child soul ties can produce lifelong insecurities in the child. This invariably results in their pursuing unhealthy relationships with others of similar personality weaknesses. At the same time, when a healthy bonding is lacking, a child may spend the rest of his or her life looking to have it fulfilled.

This is one reason why a woman will end up marrying a man who displays the same abusive tendencies as her father. Because she never properly bonded with her father, she finds herself, often without realizing it, attracted to men like her father. Why? Because she is trying to close the gap in her soul: caused by the lack of a healthy paternal soul tie. She's still trying to find his love. When a boy is not properly bonded with his father or with his mother, a similar thing happens. He'll find himself bouncing from relationship to relationship, ever seeking the deep bonding he lacked as a child. This is one of the reasons divorce is so rampant today. The 'grown up child' is trying to find the soul tie that never properly formed in the rearing years. The good news, Jesus can bring healing and restoration. David tells us in the Psalm 27:10;

Read and Write Psalm 27:10

_____

_____

_____

_____

There are two things absolutely necessary in raising children: parameters and consistency. Clearly define the rules, make sure you are consistent in enforcing them. In other words, build a fence and don't waver with the consequences when the fence is crossed. Most child-rearing problems stem from either the lack of established rules of conduct, or inconsistent insistence that the rules be observed.

Your Own Thoughts and Reflection

_____

_____

_____

_____

_____

_____

_____

_____

_____

_____

_____

_____

_____

_____

_____

_____

_____

SOUL TIES IN UNHEALTHY RELATIONSHIP

Read and Write Prov. 22:24-25

_____
_____
_____
_____
_____
_____
_____
_____

Read and Write Prov. 14:7

_____
_____
_____

Read and Write 2 Cor. 6:14-18

_____
_____
_____
_____
_____
_____
_____
_____
_____

God's Word is clearly admonished and advice in scripture to be wise in our relationships. We are told to avoid close associations with those that are angry, with those acting foolishly and with those that are unbelievers. We are not prohibited here from having *any* relationship with such persons you just do not want to make them your best of friend.

Gal 5:1 Stand fast therefore in the liberty wherewith Christ hath made us free, and be not entangled again with the yoke of bondage.

This scripture is so simple to understand, we have been made free, but He is warning us not to be entangled again with the yoke of bondage.

The word bondage means slave. We do not have to be slaves to anyone or anything.

Your Own Thoughts and Reflection

_____

_____

_____

_____

_____

_____

_____

_____

_____

_____

Judgments and Soul Ties

Read and Write Deut. 5: 16,

_____

_____

_____

_____

Read and Write Matt.7:1, 2

_____

_____

_____

_____

_____

_____

It is a principle of God that for every action, there is an equal and opposite reaction. As we study the two scriptures quoted above, we may receive some insight as to why we are experiencing problems in our lives. If we have been the victim of child abuse, for example, it is a natural response for us to feel bitter about it. What is actually occurring, however, is that our hatred and resentment toward the one who abused us may be activating a negative influence in our lives? We are judging, we are not honoring, and we are reaping the negative harvest.

It usually comes as a great surprise to many men when they discover they are just like their fathers. It is most common for an alcoholic to have an alcoholic father. Likewise, child abusers have often been abused as children.

When we can see that, a healing can take place because we can realize what our father had experienced. When we can begin to see what happened to us emotionally during our lifetime, we can understand what happened emotionally to our father during his lifetime.

If God tells us we are just like our Daddy, only worse, we can say, "'Well, now I understand why my Daddy did some of the things he did. He did them because he couldn't help it. He was an alcoholic, a sick man, just the same as I am." Many nights we went to bed wishing we weren't an alcoholic and wishing we hadn't done some of the things we did. Daddy must have done the same thing. But perhaps Daddy didn't have the opportunity to enter an alcohol and drug rehab program. Perhaps he died in his addiction, because he had no way out. This should enable us to see that God has been gracious enough to us to give us a way out. He has introduced us to this program. When we realize that, we should have no problem whatsoever forgiving Daddy. God is giving us an understanding of ourselves, and an understanding of our Daddy. Therefore, you are without excuse, every man of you who passes judgment, for in that you judge another, you condemn yourself; for you who judge practice the same things.
(Rom2:1)

In His principle concerning judgment, God declares that when we live in an ongoing judgmental attitude, we are captured by that attitude and we become what we are judging. What has happened is that we have become focused upon a sin issue rather than upon our Lord Jesus Christ, and whatever we focus upon becomes the driving dynamic force in our lives. That is why we often find that what we hate in our parents becomes evident in our lives, also.

Do not be deceived, God is not mocked; for whatever a man sows, this he will also reap. **(Galatians 6:7)**

Whatever judgments we sow against another, we will receive from others. Knowing this, we should desire to sow love and mercy wherever we go knowing we will receive love and mercy in return.

In the matter of healing hidden root judgments, we should look at healing the root causes of the problems in our inner man. If we have a bitter root expectation that we will fail, we will find ourselves constantly failing. If we have a bitter root expectation of being rejected, we will bring rejection upon ourselves.

Whatever is incubated within our souls is created in our circumstances. Whatever we project out through our souls to others is received by their souls and sent back to us. For this reason, we should keep our souls soaked in Divine love.

"And the axe is already laid at the root of the trees; every tree therefore that does not bear good fruit is cut down and thrown into the fire.(**Matthew 3: 10**)

In dealing with the heart, we must allow God to go deep into the roots of our heart's attitudes, motivations and character traits. He will do this as we commune with Him during our quiet time. He will reveal our motives by asking us why we want to do a certain thing. He will expose poor attitudes, and challenge us to allow Him to heal them with His love.

Your Own Thoughts and Reflection

_____

_____

_____

_____

_____

_____

_____

_____

_____

_____

_____

_____

_____

_____

_____

_____

_____

_____

1. How can we establish good soul ties?

_____
_____
_____
_____
_____
_____
_____
_____
_____
_____
_____
_____
_____
_____
_____
_____
_____
_____
_____
_____
_____
_____
_____

2. How are evil soul ties established?

_____

_____

_____

_____

_____

_____

_____

_____

_____

_____

_____

_____

_____

_____

_____

_____

_____

_____

_____

_____

_____

_____

_____

_____

3. When the proper parent/child soul tie isn't established, what happens?

_____

_____

_____

_____

_____

_____

_____

_____

_____

_____

_____

_____

_____

_____

_____

_____

_____

_____

_____

_____

_____

4. How can family soul ties become perverted?

_____
_____
_____
_____
_____
_____
_____
_____
_____
_____
_____
_____
_____
_____
_____
_____
_____
_____
_____
_____
_____
_____
_____
_____
_____

5. In what way does judging, sowing and reaping bring similar results?

_____

_____

_____

_____

_____

_____

_____

_____

_____

_____

_____

_____

_____

_____

_____

_____

_____

_____

_____

_____

_____

6. Why is it important to be specific when breaking soul ties, or when asking God's forgiveness for being judgmental?

_____

_____

_____

_____

_____

_____

_____

_____

_____

_____

_____

_____

_____

_____

_____

_____

_____

_____

_____

_____

_____

_____

Chapter 3

The Breaking of Evil Soul Ties

And Prayers

Read and Write John 8:31-32

_____
_____
_____
_____
_____
_____
_____
_____
_____
_____
_____
_____

Read and Write John 8: 36

_____
_____
_____
_____
_____
_____
_____
_____

Read and Write Rom 8:15, 16

_____

_____

_____

_____

_____

_____

_____

_____

_____

_____

Read and Write Gal 5:1

_____

_____

_____

_____

_____

_____

_____

_____

_____

_____

_____

_____

_____

These scriptures above are telling us that we have been set free, if we have made Jesus the Lord of our life, because whom the son sets free is free indeed. Remember God's Word is truth, and the truth sets us free.

In Romans 8:15 and 16 says we did not receive the spirit of bondage, but we received the spirit of adoption. We were adopted as children of God and have the right to call Him Abba Father.

Your Own Thoughts and Reflection

_____

_____

_____

_____

_____

_____

_____

_____

_____

_____

_____

_____

_____

_____

_____

_____

THE BREAKING OF EVIL SOUL TIES

1. Almightily God, one and true living God, I ask forgiveness for the sin of fornication and sexual immorality with the following list of people, in the name of Jesus Christ.

2. When I speak out their name and bring their face into my mind, and you forgive me, I will also forgive myself, allowing no shame, quilt or condemnation to come on me or remain in me. I pray you would wash me and all my body parts in the blood of the lamb so as to cleanse me and my mind. Please also dear Lord Jesus Christ, remove all memories of the sins as you restore me to wholeness.

3. Ask the Holy Spirit to bring to mind breaking every person you need to break soul ties with. If you cannot remember their name (i.e. prostitute or far back in memory) then say "Lord you know who this person is. I break the soul tie with that person now in the name of Jesus Christ." Work through each person slowly. Here is a sample prayer:

4. I ask forgiveness for the sin of fornication and or sexual immortality with (name of person). I ask forgiveness for all ways in which I hurt that person during our relationship and I forgive all ways that person hurt me. Heal me in these areas now Lord Jesus Christ, I break all one flesh relationships and sever all soul ties, physical, emotional, mental, sexual and psychic. I ask the Lord Jesus Christ that all parts of me would came back to me now, washed in the blood of the lamb, and I send all parts of them back to them, washed in the blood of the lamb. I pray also that you would now close all doors or entry points forever in the name of Jesus Christ, including all objects of mine that they have and all objects of them that I have. I plead the blood of Jesus Christ over those objects removing legal rights to harass me and I ask that you would pull out all sexual hooks from me and them.

REPEAT THIS PRAYER WITH EVERY PERSON THE HOLY SPIRIT BRINGS TO MIND.

RESTORING THE FRAGMENTED SOUL

In the name of the Lord Jesus Christ, I break all bondages over my conscious and unconscious mind. I ask God to send out His' angels to gather all portion of my mind that have been removed by Witchcraft, Communism, Masonry, any Occult or Witchcraft Practices, False Religions, Demonic Music, Drugs, Alcohol and by any other means, to be restored to me now.

Read and Write Ps 23, 3

_____

_____

_____

_____

Read and Write Ps. 7:1

_____

_____

_____

_____

_____

_____

Read and Write Ps.35:15

_____

_____

_____

_____

Read and Write Job 33:10

_____
_____
_____
_____
_____
_____
_____
_____
_____

Read and Write Ezek. 13:17

_____
_____
_____
_____

Your Own Thoughts and Reflection

_____
_____
_____
_____
_____
_____
_____
_____
_____

Almightily God, one and true living God, I break and renounce all evil soul ties I have ever had or may have had with {name any Masonic lodges, adulterer, close friends, ex-spouses, cults, binding agreements between buddies, etc.}. I renounce all evil soul ties, break then and declare them destroyed by the blood of the Lord Jesus Christ. In the name of Jesus Christ I now renounce, break and loose myself from all demonic subjection to my mother, father grandparents or any other human being, living or dead, who has dominated me in any way which is contrary to the will of God. I thank you Lord Jesus Christ, for setting me free. I command all demons to be bound and cast out. I ask you, Almightily God, one and true living God, to send angels to uncoil, untangle, dig out, break, sever off and remove all demons and demonic roots. Also all fetters, bands, ties, bonds, coils, tangles, serpents, cords in the name of Jesus Christ. Almightily God, I ask that the angels gather and restore the fragments of my soul (mind, will and emotions) to their rightful place in me, In the name of the Lord Jesus Christ, I ask for angels to unearth and break all earthen vessels, cut bonds, band and bindings that have been put upon my soul, willingly or without my knowledge.

I ask that the angels free my soul from all bondages by whatever means is required. I agree and declare, Almighty God, that the power of the Lord Jesus Christ is all powerful and effective to do this. I ask this that my soul might fully magnify and glorify the Lord Jesus Christ.

Your Own Thoughts and Reflection

Prayer Breaking Un-godly Soul-Ties

Father God in the name of Jesus I renounce all covenants, pacts, promises, curses and every other work of darkness to which I have been exposed or made liable by my own actions or by the actions of others.

By the act and decision of my own free will, Father, in the name of Jesus,

I ask You to go to the root and dig, cut, tear and loose me from every soul-tie and from every form of bondage of my soul and body to Satan, or any of his agents rather in human form or demonic form or animal form.

And Father, in the name of Jesus, I also, ask that You go to each of the above named, and at the root, dig, tear, cut and loose them from me.

Take and separate me out of them, and separate them from and out of me, in Jesus name!

I choose now to present my body to the Lord, as a living sacrifice, as the scriptures recommend, and to walk in holiness as You, Lord Jesus, enable me to do so.

Pray, Take Authority and Cast Out Spirits

Mark 16:17

And these signs shall follow them that believe; In my name they shall cast out devils.

In the name of Jesus, I take authority over the spirits tormenting me. You spirit's) of _____ (name them), I command you to be broken and leave me, come out! Right now, in Jesus name. Amen.

I command every portion of my soul (my thoughts, my will, my emotions, my personality and mind) and heart, all of me: spirit, soul and body, that has been fragmented, torn or broken or cursed, to come back into its proper place; and to be healed; every piece of my heart to be returned; my soul to be restored and every bondage and related soul-tie to be completely broken, destroyed and totally disconnected from me, in the name of Jesus!

Father God, in the name of Jesus, I ask now, that You heal my heart and guard it by Your Power and Your Love, and keep my heart and mind through Christ Jesus.

Make me every whole in every area of my life.

I desire to live in a manner that pleases You and brings glory to Your name.

Your Own Thoughts and Reflection

Prayer Confession

In the name of Jesus Christ of Nazareth, I hereby, renounce and revoke any and all vows that I have made (intentionally or un-intentionally), with knowledge of or in ignorance.

I take back the words I spoke and said to these people: (name them) (marriage vows or any others)

I also break any soul-ties consequential from any vows I made, and take authority over any evil spirits sent to re-enforce any vows or to torment me. I command you to be broken, and to leave me right now, in Jesus name. Amen.

I am free! In Jesus name! Thank You, Lord!

Thank You Jesus for Saving and Delivering me!

Breaking Curses

In the name of the Lord Jesus Christ of Nazareth, by the power of His blood, His cross and His resurrection, I take authority over all curses, hexes, spells, voodoo practices, witchcraft assignments, satanic rituals, incantations and evil wishes that have been sent my way, sent my family way or have passed down the generational bloodline. I break all forms of demonic oppression and influence over my life and my family lives by the power of the risen Lord Jesus Christ, and I ask that all curses be replaced with a blessing.

I ask forgiveness for and denounce all negative inner vows and agreements that I have made with the enemy, and I ask that you Lord Jesus Christ release me from any bondage they may have held in me. I claim your shed blood over all aspects of my life and my family lives, relationships, ministry endeavors and finances. I thank you for your enduring love, your angelic protection, and for the fullness of your abundant blessings.

Pray for love ones to be set free from cults.....

"Father in the name of Jesus, I come before You in prayer and in faith believing that Your Word runs swiftly throughout the earth for the Word of God is not chained or imprisoned. I bring before You _____ (*those and families of those involved in cults*). Father God, stretch forth Your hand from above, rescue and deliver _____ out of great waters, from the land of hostile aliens whose mouth speaks deceit and whose right hand is a right hand raised in taking fraudulent oaths. Their mouths must be stopped for they are mentally distressing and subverting_____ and whole families by teaching what they ought not teach, for the purpose of getting base advantage and disreputable gain. But praise God, they will not get very far for their rash folly will become obvious to everyone!

"Execute justice, precious Father, for the oppressed. Set the prisoners free, open the eyes of the blind, lift up the bowed down, heal the brokenhearted, bind up their wounds curing their pains and sorrow. Lift up the humble and down- trodden and cast the wicked down to the ground in the mighty name of Jesus."

"Turn back the hearts of the disobedient, incredulous, and un-persuadable to the wisdom of the upright, the knowledge, and holy love of the will of God in order to make ready for You, Lord a people perfectly prepared in spirit, adjusted, disposed, and placed in the right moral state.

"Father God, You say in Your Word to refrain our voice from weeping and our eyes from tears for our prayers shall be rewarded and _____ shall return from the enemy's land and come again to their own country. You will save our offspring from the land of their exile, from the east and the west- sons from afar and daughter from the ends of the earth. I shall see _____ walking in the ways of piety and virtue revering Your name, Father God in the name of Jesus. Those who err in spirit will come to understanding. Those who murmur discontentedly will accept instruction in the Way, Jesus. Father God You contend with those who contend with us and You give safety to _____and ease_____."

"SATEN, I SPEAK TO YOU IN THE NAME OF JESUS. I BIND YOU, THE PRINCIPALITIES, THE POWERS, THE RULERS OF THE DARKNESS AND THE WICKED SPIRITS IN HEAVENLY PLACES, AND I TEAR DOWN STRONGHOLDS USING THE MIGHY WEAPONS GOD HAS PROVIDED FOR US IN THE NAME OF JESUS. I SPEAK TO GREED, SELFISHNESS, PRIDE, ARROGANCE, BOASTFULNESS, ABUSE, BLASPHEMY, DISORBEDIENCE, UNGRAREFUL, PROFANITY, REBELLION, PERVERSENESS, SLANDER, IMMORALITY, FEROCITY, HATRED,, TREACHERY, CONCEIT, LUST, MATERIALISM, ERROR, DECEIT, SPIRIT OF ANTICHRIST, ERROR, DECEIT, SPIRIT OF HOSTILITY, DEPRAVITY, DISTORTION, UNGODLINESS, AND FALSITY AND LOOSE YOUFROM ALL DIABOLICAL ASSIGMENTS AGAINST_____ I CANCEL ALL NEGATIVE TALKING AND DOUBT AND UNBELIEF. SATAN WILL NOT USE THIS AGAINST _____."

I commission the ministering spirit to go forth and dispel these forces of darkness and bring _____ home in the name of Jesus."

"Father God, I believe and confess that _____
Has had knowledge of and been acquainted with the Word which was able to instruct _____
and give _____the understanding for salvation which comes through faith in Christ Jesus. Lord I pray and believe that You certainly will deliver _____and draw and bring them into Your heavenly kingdom. Glory to You, Father God who delivers those for whom I intercede in for in Jesus' name. Amen."

Once this has been prayed for an individual, confess it as done. Thank the Father that the person is delivered, returning from the enemy's land. Thank God that Satan is bound and thank God for the person salvation.

Prayer for the Home

"Father, I thank You that You have blessed me with all spiritual blessings in Christ Jesus.

"Through skillful and godly wisdom is my house (my life, established on a sound and good foundation. And by knowledge shall the chambers (of its every area) be filled with all precious and pleasant riches – great priceless treasure. The house of the uncompromisingly righteous shall stand. Prosperity and welfare are in my house in the name of Jesus.

"My house is securely build. It is found on a rock, revelation knowledge of Your Word Father. Jesus is my Cornerstone; Jesus is Lord of my household; Jesus is Lord over _____ our spirit, soul and body.

"Whatever may be our task we work at it heartily as something done for You Lord, and not for men. We love each other with the God kind of love, and we dwell in peace. My home is deposited into Your charge, entrusted to Your protection and care.

"Father as for me and my house we shall serve the Lord in Jesus' name, Hallelujah!"

Prayer for Safety

"Father God, in the name of Jesus, I thank You that You watch over Your Word to perform it. I thank You that I dwell in the secret place of the Most High and I remain stable and fixed under the shadow of the Almighty whose power no foe can withstand."

"Father God, You are my refuge and my fortress. No evil shall befall me – no accident shall overtake me – nor any plague or calamity come near my home. You give Your angels special charge over me, to accompany and defend and preserve me in all my ways of obedience and service. They are encamped around and about me."

"Father God, You are my confidence, firm and strong. You keep my foot from being caught in a trap or hidden danger. Father, You give me safety and ease me – Jesus is my safety!

Write your own Prayers

_____
_____
_____
_____
_____
_____
_____
_____
_____
_____
_____
_____
_____
_____
_____
_____
_____
_____
_____
_____
_____
_____
_____
_____
_____
_____
_____

Your Own Thoughts and Reflection

CPSIA information can be obtained at www.ICGtesting.com
Printed in the USA
LVOW081721280612

288085LV00010B/73/P

9 781450 763615